D1055248

BEING FEMALE **IN AMERICA**

GROWING UP A GIRL

BY DUCHESS HARRIS, JD, PHD
WITH NANCY REDD

Essential Library

An Imprint of Abdo Publishing | abdopublishing.com

ABDOPUBLISHING.COM

Published by Abdo Publishing, a division of ABDO, PO Box 398166, Minneapolis, Minnesota 55439. Copyright © 2018 by Abdo Consulting Group, Inc. International copyrights reserved in all countries. No part of this book may be reproduced in any form without written permission from the publisher. Essential Library™ is a trademark and logo of Abdo Publishing.

Printed in the United States of America, North Mankato, Minnesota
092017
012018

THIS BOOK CONTAINS RECYCLED MATERIALS

Cover Photo: Shutterstock Images
Interior Photos: iStockphoto, 4–5, 10, 23, 28–29, 44, 46–47, 48, 60, 68–69, 86–87, 92–93; Money Business Images/Shutterstock Images, 13; World History Archive/Newscom, 14–15; Lisa F. Young/Shutterstock Images, 16; Erik McGregor/Sipa USA/AP Images, 18–19; Shutterstock Images, 20–21, 42, 65, 72–73; Gagliardi Images/Shutterstock Images, 30, 97; Yuri Arcurs/iStockphoto, 32–33; Africa Studio/Shutterstock Images, 35; Dan Honda/TNS/Newscom, 54; Money Business Images/iStockphoto, 58–59, 80–81; Solis Images/Shutterstock Images, 77; Romuald Meigneux/Sipa/AP Images, 78; Vince Bucci/Invision/AP Images, 83; Jeff Malet Photography/Newscom, 90–91; Alex J. Berliner/AP Images, 95

Editor: Alyssa Krekelberg
Series Designer: Maggie Villaume

PUBLISHER'S CATALOGING-IN-PUBLICATION DATA

Names: Harris, Duchess, author. | Redd, Nancy, author.
Title: Growing up a girl / by Duchess Harris and Nancy Redd.
Description: Minneapolis, Minnesota : Abdo Publishing, 2018. | Series: Being female in America |
Identifiers: LCCN 2017946730 | ISBN 9781532113062 (lib.bdg.) | ISBN 9781532151941 (ebook)
Subjects: LCSH: Teenage girls--United States--Juvenile literature. | Social media--Juvenile literature. | Social life and customs--Juvenile literature. | Teenage girls--Conduct of life--Juvenile literature.
Classification: DDC 305.235--dc23
LC record available at https://lccn.loc.gov/2017946730

CONTENTS

CHAPTER ONE

DRESS CODE
DRAMA

Kaitlyn Juvik went braless for her entire senior year at Helena High School in Montana. She, along with many of her friends, felt bras were uncomfortable, restrictive, and unnecessary. In May 2016, despite the absence of a bra requirement in the school dress code, the vice principal reprimanded Kaitlyn for not wearing a bra.

Kaitlyn had previously worn the same loose-fitting black top to school with no issues. Still, the vice principal told Kaitlyn she needed to put on a bra because not wearing one might make the male teachers and students feel uncomfortable.

Kaitlyn believes girls should not have to wear bras "as long as nothing is showing and you're covered up." Later, she shared with a Montana news outlet, "The fact that I was told that [my natural body] makes people uncomfortable offended me. . . . I'm not sure why that is uncomfortable to somebody."[1]

Kaitlyn complained about the interaction on social media, where she posted a picture of herself in the offending shirt, saying it was "not see through, not inappropriate and you definitely cannot tell I'm not wearing a bra unless you're looking very hard."[2] She received the support of many fellow students, both male and female. Because of this, Kaitlyn created a

Facebook page called "No Bra, No Problem." She and other Helena High students decided to organize "no bra day." They wanted this movement to help others in their community understand the importance of gender equality and not sexualizing women's bodies.

On "no bra day," Steve Thennis, the school principal, pulled Kaitlyn into the office multiple times to ask her to stop being a distraction to people by encouraging women to go braless. Kaitlyn, however, had the opposite viewpoint. She said it was the principal who was distracting from her learning by making her meet with him during class, just because the girls were not wearing an article of clothing they didn't like and that was not mandatory. "We're always asked to do things to

IS SOCIAL MEDIA THE SOLUTION?

"I think we live in a culture that's so used to looking at issues of harassment and assault through the wrong end of the telescope," says Laura Bates, a cofounder of the Everyday Sexism Project. "There's a real culture being built up through some of these dress codes where girls are receiving very clear messages that male behavior, male entitlement to your body in public space is socially acceptable, but you will be punished." But Bates has hope for the next generation. "We've seen a real resurgence in the popularity of feminism and feminist activism, particularly among young people and particularly in an international sense, facilitated by social media." To Bates, dress code protests are an example of this comeback, citing how today's girls have the "courage to tackle the forms of sexism that are very subtle, that previously it was very difficult to stand up to, because you would be accused of overreacting, of making a fuss out of nothing."[3]

GIRLS BANNED FROM FLIGHTS

Rules and regulations around the appropriateness of clothing are evidence of gender inequality for girls growing up in the United States. In 2017, two teenage girls were trying to board a United Airlines flight. They were traveling on employee passes. The passes required the travelers to follow a dress code. The girls were denied boarding and missed their flight because they were wearing leggings. The gate agent decided the girls were not "properly clothed" for a flight.[6] A third girl, just ten years old, was denied boarding until she put on a dress over her leggings. A bystander took to social media to post her frustration about the situation. United defended its position, saying it had the "right to refuse transport" and that "there is a dress code" for certain travelers.[7] But people were still outraged by the sexism shown toward young girls in terms of what is and is not appropriate for flight.

make guys more comfortable," Kaitlyn wrote in a newspaper op-ed. "If my boobs make you uncomfortable, then why are you looking at me in that way?"[4]

Kaitlyn's actions went viral. People around the world chimed in on whether bras should be mandatory in school. Many young women staged their own "no bra day" and shared pictures of themselves using the hashtag #NoBraNoProblem. Principal Thennis, however, did not publicly change his opinion, saying that even though the dress code rules did not mention undergarments, he was "done talking about it" and that Kaitlyn had "created a manufactured crisis."[5]

But Kaitlyn was not done talking about it. To her and the thousands of women and men worldwide who supported her, this was about much more than just a bra. "This is about ending body shaming," Kaitlyn wrote. "This is about ending double standards for girls."[8]

DOUBLE STANDARDS DEFINED

Double standards are embedded into American society. When a boy takes charge, he's being a boss. But when a girl is in control, she's being bossy. If a man goes on lots of dates, he is complimented by his peers. But if a woman does the same, she's viewed as sexually promiscuous. A man going topless on the beach is normal, whereas a woman in the United States can be fined or even jailed for baring her breasts in public.

These common real-life examples embody the double standards set for girls and boys. Double standards are sets of principles that are applied differently and more strictly to one group of people than to another. Starting from birth, most girls are faced with double standards that shape how they feel about their personal capabilities, self-worth, and physical beauty. How boys view girls in relationship to themselves is also shaped by these double standards, and not just during youth. For example, boys who grow up thinking girls who are in control are bossy might not want to work underneath or promote women. Sexist practices in adulthood, such as not wanting to trust

Stereotypes about girls, including that they're being bossy if they're assertive, begin at a young age.

in or vote for a woman, and the hypersexualization of the female body, start with double standards set early in life.

Because men still retain much of the social power in the United States, women's issues are often marginalized, meaning that they are not considered important enough to spend time and effort solving. Many men, and some women, in positions of power do not believe there are double standards. Or if they do acknowledge sexist behaviors exist, often they do not see anything wrong with the practices. Many sexist practices are rooted in American tradition and intersect with cultural morals and values. Women and men who advocate for change by fighting against double standards and sexism are often labeled as attention seeking, troublemaking, and difficult, as Kaitlyn and her peers were.

SEXISM THEN AND NOW

Sexism is the unfair discrimination against people because of their gender. Men and boys can suffer from sexism, too. For centuries,

RACIALIZED SEXISM

Cultural stereotypes, beauty ideals, and racism in the United States mean that girls and women of color experience sexism differently. They also experience it in ways that are often invisible to women and men who are not of the same background. Race and gender are inseparable, and the intersection, or combination, should not be ignored. Racialized sexism is when race and gender intersect to create a unique set of issues surrounding gender and racial inequality. For example, schools frequently enact dress codes that ban common African-American hairstyles like afro puffs or braids because administrators see them as "extreme" or "distracting."[9] The policies don't allow for hairstyles that are culturally different from a perceived white norm. Studies show that Hispanic and African-American girls are more likely to be disciplined for dress code violations and that their punishments are harsher than those given to white students.

women in the United States did not have the right to vote, own property, or go to Ivy League colleges. Birth control, divorce, working while pregnant, and many other aspects of modern life were restricted for women until the latter half of the 1900s. Participating in certain sports, including soccer and long-distance running, was considered unsuitable for the female body until the 1970s. Until that same decade, women were legally prevented from having their own credit cards. For minority women, the intersectionality of race and gender meant it often took even longer for them to access the opportunities eventually afforded to white women.

Today, all girls and women in the United States have these rights, and many others, because of the push for equality that started in the 1800s. During this time, some men and women around the world started fighting for the political, social, and economic equality of

WHAT IS INTERSECTIONALITY?

Intersectionality refers to the different ways discrimination can overlap based on a person's class, sex, race, sexuality, and ability. This shapes a person's privileges and disadvantages, affects how he or she is perceived and treated by others, and can contribute to discrimination and unequal treatment. For example, a lesbian girl growing up in a wealthy household and a low-income heterosexual disabled girl might both be white, but their life experiences and challenges will likely be very different. Acknowledging a person's intersectionality helps to break down communication barriers and champion equality for all.

In 1972, a law called Title IX helped bridge the gender gap between girls' and boys' sports. Today, girls have more opportunities to play sports than they did in the past.

Women's rights activists protested at the Republican National Convention in 1920 to support the Nineteenth Amendment, which passed later that year.

the sexes. Many of these activists were, and still are, called feminists.

For more than a century, feminists have worked to shape laws, customs, and beliefs in the United States to be more equal and fair. They worked to redefine human rights to include women as equal to men. The first goal of feminists was to band together and solidify women as citizens with the right to vote alongside men. After more than 70 years of activism, they accomplished this goal with the passing of the Nineteenth Amendment in 1920. Over time, feminism has shifted and evolved, with each wave building upon prior victories. Feminists continue to fight for gender equality and to better define the acts and actions that are considered sexist towards women. Without definitions of sexism, it would be impossible to explain what is wrong about it and how it harms girls and women.

Modern-day sexism is more subtle than the sexism experienced by previous generations. The battles over the right for

Sexism at school can have a negative impact on girls' education.

girls to attend school or enter the workforce have been resolved legally. Girls have the same legal rights as boys, and theoretically the same opportunities, but there are many aspects to sexism that are difficult to make illegal. For example, the smaller, more subjective issues, such as catcalling or dress codes, might seem like no big deal. From school teachers to hiring managers, many people may be aware of sexist practices and behaviors but find nothing wrong with them. Other people may not even be aware of their sexist attitudes and beliefs until they are called out on their actions.

Eliminating sexism and promoting gender equality requires not only awareness but also action. Inactivity and silence on the rights that matter most to a person can easily cause those rights to be taken away. It is not enough to believe in the concept of equality. An enlightened person must take time to educate those around him or her and fight for what is fair. This requires knowledge of the United States' complicated history, alertness to present struggles, and a passion to see an even brighter future.

DISCUSSION STARTERS

- Do you think the vice principal's request that Kaitlyn Juvik put on a bra was sexist? If you aren't certain, what additional information would you need to make your decision?
- What acts of sexism have you recently witnessed? Do you think they were intentional?
- What privileges and disadvantages stem from your own intersectionality? How has it shaped you and how people perceive you?

IS FEMINISM
STILL NEEDED?

Feminism is evolving. Since the mid-2000s, social media and the Internet have allowed feminists worldwide to join together in support of equality. However, a lack of awareness regarding the history of sexism has impacted today's girls in a way that previous generations of activists did not expect. Because of the opportunities afforded them, many young women and men believe in the equality of the sexes. But they do not consider themselves feminists. Some people subscribe to the ideas and beliefs of feminism but do not want to be labeled as feminists. The once-proud badge of feminist has been tarnished by people who equate feminism with hating men, and the term is often considered outdated or negative. Because of this, it's not just the term *feminist* that is losing power but also progress.

In only a few generations, centuries of fighting against inequality have brought girls and women to the brink of true equality. But women still face issues. Today, numerous politicians do not believe pay equality

Women marched down New York City streets to celebrate International Women's Day, which promotes gender equality.

between men and women is a problem, even though women do not receive the same pay as men for the same work. In addition, they do not support paid maternity and paternity leave or other programs that would make it easier for women to support their families.

CHAPTER TWO

WHAT IS
"GIRL STUFF"?

Starting at a young age, girls are conditioned to favor stereotypically feminine objects, such as dollhouses and tea sets.

At a restaurant, when a parent orders a kids' meal that comes with a toy, the cashier might ask, "Boy or girl?" Instead of focusing on a child's preference, buyers will often purchase toys, bedding, clothes, and even snack foods according to stereotypical concepts of gender. "Girl" items tend to be pink or pastel with dainty female characters, while "boy" things are bold in color and prominently feature muscular men.

In 2015, a viral tweet shamed a Target store for having a toy-aisle sign that separated building toys for girls away from other building toys. Target then announced its decision to remove gender-specific signs from its toy department, saying that labeling products based on gender was unnecessary for its customers.

Many people were excited to shop for kids' toys without being forced into a stereotypical

THE PINK TAX

Gender-specific products cost women more because of price discrimination. A recent study in New York City found that products marketed to girls and women cost on average 7 percent more than comparable products for boys and men.[1] Activists refer to this price discrimination as the pink tax. The tax covers everything from clothing to toys to services, but personal care items are especially costly for women. Women's razors can cost up to double the price of razors marketed for men, even if the only difference is the color. Some companies and organizations are working to equalize prices and bring awareness to the issue, but people can avoid falling prey to price discrimination by making purchase decisions by price instead of by gender norms.

Pink has been labeled a feminine color.

gender-specific aisle. But there were some who expressed anger with Target for choosing to support gender neutrality over decades of traditional cultural norms in the United States. One angry shopper wrote, "Gender neutral is ridiculous . . . pink has always been for girls [and] blue has always been for boys."[2] But according to historian Jo B. Paoletti, assigned gender-specific colors didn't always exist.

Paoletti is the author of *Pink and Blue: Telling the Boys from the Girls in America*. Her research explores how clothing and colors in the United States have evolved from being unisex, or gender neutral, to exclusively male or female. According to Paoletti, pink has been a "girl" color since the 1940s. Before that, not only did boys wear pink, but it was actually the preferred color for males. It was deemed stronger and less dainty than the color blue.

In addition to gendered colors, clothes for men and women have also changed throughout history. In 1884, when President Franklin Roosevelt was a young boy, he took a formal portrait wearing a fancy white dress, just like other boys did during his time. Men wore high heels for centuries before they became popular as women's footwear. Today, as in the past, shifts are happening in what is designated and culturally appreciated as "girl" and "boy" stuff. Many of these changes are swinging back toward a more universal and less gendered experience. One example is the names parents give their children. Gender-neutral names, such as Phoenix or Reese, are becoming more popular and trendy. BabyCenter.com's Linda Murray says it reflects "a larger cultural shift" because some modern parents do not want their children to be restricted or stereotyped.[3]

BIOLOGY OF THE FEMALE BODY

At birth, a child is assigned a biological sex of either female or male. Visually, biological sex is determined by external genitalia. A biological female has a vulva while a biological male possesses a penis. Internally,

TOO FRAGILE TO RUN?

While the majority of marathon runners today are women, well into the 1960s marathons were only for men. Gender norms at the time discouraged women from "unladylike" sports such as running. Inaccurate information about biology led many to perceive the female body as too fragile to run long distances.

In 1967, runner Kathrine Switzer was tired of being excluded because of false gender expectations. She became the first woman to officially enter the Boston Marathon, registering under "K. V. Switzer," a name that concealed her gender. Once she was on the course, however, her anonymity was over. While her fellow runners and the media were excited to see a woman competing, the marathon officials were appalled. A few miles into the race, the race director began to follow her, verbally threatening her and physically assaulting her as he tried to push her off the course. After her boyfriend and fellow runner pushed the director away, Switzer persevered and became the first woman to officially finish the marathon.

hormones, organs, and chromosomes help to determine biological sex.

Up until the 1700s, females were thought of medically as imperfect males. By creating a hierarchy between males and females based purely on biological differences, men were able to exert control over women for centuries. They deemed women to be incompetent and ineligible for a variety of roles within society solely because of their sex. Until the last century it was almost impossible to debunk the long-standing belief that females were the inferior sex. This was primarily because all of the scientists, doctors, and scholars on the topic were males. Higher education and other activities outside of the home were often frowned upon for girls and women.

Slowly, laws and cultural practices changed, enabling more females to become educated and influential. This sparked more research on the differences between the sexes, making it clearer that while males and females are not the same biologically, their differences are not necessarily better or worse, but complementary.

GENDER NORMS

While a person's sex is biological, gender is largely a social construct. This means that expected male and female behaviors can be different based on culture. For example, in Scotland men wear skirts called kilts to weddings, Scottish dance parties, or other special occasions. In India, men who are just friends often hold hands. These are examples of expressions of gender that are considered unusual in the United States but are perfectly normal elsewhere.

Just as with gender-assigned colors, people in the United States tend to look at social constructs of gender as innate, or something girls and boys are born with. In actuality, gender norms are a set of learned behaviors. The reason many people think of gender identity as innate is because people are bombarded with gender norms from birth. Once learned, these norms become internalized and integral to how people think. These norms can become so rooted within people that it's impossible for them to imagine a world where girls don't all want to wear pink and boys don't all

GENDER IDENTITY

Gender is not just what society expects of a male or female but also how a person sees herself or himself, as well as how she or he presents to the world. Most people are cisgender, meaning that their gender identity matches up with their assigned biological sex. Sometimes a person's gender identity does not match their assigned sex, and they identify as transgender. A transgender girl might have been assigned the male sex at birth, but her gender identity is female. Often transgender people change outward signs of their gender, such as their name, clothing, or hair, to match their gender identities. Some transgender people seek medical help as part of their transition to match their gender identities. It is important to note that gender and sex are separate from sexual orientation. A transgender person can be sexually attracted to women, men, both, or neither.

want to play football. However, a century ago it was nearly impossible to imagine a world where women could vote and own property and men could change diapers or stay at home with the children.

Even gender norms that seem harmless and fun, such as depicting certain activities and behaviors as feminine or masculine, can have long-term negative effects. "Our ideas of what constitutes a real man or woman are not natural; they are restrictive norms that are harmful to children of both genders," says Dr. Maria do Mar Pereira, a sociologist at the University of Warwick in England. She spent three months shadowing a class of eighth graders to study the effect of gender roles. She found that because girls are so worried about fitting into gender norms of femininity, they "downplay their own abilities, pretending to be less intelligent than they actually are, not speaking out against harassment, and withdrawing from hobbies, sports and activities that might seem 'unfeminine.'"[4]

Children learn gender norms from the adults around them.

Both girls and boys can experience bullying.

Despite pushback from previous generations, norms are changing with a growing awareness of entrenched gender expectations. Pereira interviewed a classroom of teenagers as part of a study on gender norms. Both traditionally masculine and feminine teens and nonconforming kids said they were unhappy about having to pay so much attention to behaving according to masculine and feminine gender role expectations. But they all assumed there was no alternative. When Pereira made the teenagers aware of gender traits as performance, and not as inherently biological traits, she found that bullies mocked their peers for acting in nontraditional gendered ways less frequently than before. Additionally, girls and boys integrated more, and physical fights decreased. "Sometimes adults think it's impossible to change gender norms because they're already so deeply entrenched," Pereira said in an interview. "But they're much more entrenched in adults than they are in young people."[5]

DISCUSSION STARTERS

- Do you think Target made a good decision to make its toy department gender neutral? Why or why not?
- What are some gender norms you notice in your community? Do you disagree with any of the gender norms you see? Explain your reasoning.
- Do you agree that gender identity is created by society? Why or why not?

CHAPTER THREE

SELF-ESTEEM
& BODY IMAGE

While the terms *body image* and *self-esteem* are often
used interchangeably, they describe different aspects of
a person's self-image. Self-esteem is the level of respect
that a person has for himself or herself. A teen girl with
high levels of self-esteem tends to be confident and
comfortable with herself, while a girl with low levels
of self-esteem usually does not think very highly of her
abilities and can be insecure about her appearance. A
person's level of self-esteem is that person's self-rating of
his or her intelligence, social standing, talent, and physical
appearance, which is where body image comes into play.

Body image is the way a person thinks about his or her
physical appearance. While body image is only one facet of
a girl's self-esteem, it is often the most important factor.
This is due to gender norms and societal expectations, as
women are often expected to adhere to narrow standards
of beauty, weight, and sex appeal.

The National Institute on Media and Family reports
that by the time girls are 13 years old, 53 percent are
"unhappy with their bodies." By the time girls are 17 years
old, the figure grows to 78 percent.[1] This unhappiness
can lower girls' self-esteem. It can also create a domino
effect that can damage a girl's financial, academic, and
relationship success. Girls with low self-esteem spend

The cosmetics industry makes billions of dollars each year as many women try to meet society's beauty standards by wearing makeup.

tremendous amounts of money on products and services that promise to fix their problems. Girls who feel bad about their looks often skip school or avoid other social activities. They also tend to have more unsafe sex and unhealthy relationships and are much more likely to harm themselves by smoking, drinking, self-mutilating, or engaging in disordered eating.

Raising a person's level of self-esteem isn't as simple as getting a makeover or losing weight. Self-esteem and body image are complicated issues. How a girl feels about herself often has little to do with reality and everything to do with her perception of reality. Intersectionality also plays a huge role in self-esteem levels. Class, race, sexuality, religion, and other defining characteristics can all move the self-esteem needle in a positive

SEXINESS ON KIDS' TV SHOWS

Sexualized beauty ideals are perpetuated by the media. Children's television shows have been found to influence body image ideals and hypersexuality in the little girls who watch them. Recently, the Geena Davis Institute on Gender in Media analyzed thousands of speaking characters in family-friendly and children's programming. Nearly one-third of the female characters were wearing sexy attire, compared to less than 10 percent of the males.[2] Not only do these sexualized images affect girls and their self-esteem, but they give boys who watch these shows unrealistic and inappropriate expectations for how girls should look, dress, and behave. These messages become ingrained in boys and girls from an early age. Once these messages are solidified as gender norms, they become difficult to change.

or negative direction, depending on how people feel about these aspects of themselves.

Across the country there are girls and women who have high levels of self-esteem and body confidence because they have successfully rejected gender norms and beauty ideals. They focus on appreciating and accepting themselves as individuals with unique sets of talents and gifts. Conversely, there are millions of girls suffering from low levels of self-esteem and poor body image. Women and girls spend years internalizing negative images from the mainstream media, which often creates a mental state in which women and girls believe they can never be pretty or thin enough.

IMPOSSIBLE STANDARDS

One key reason girls in the United States negatively critique their bodies is because society's standard of beauty is impossible to achieve naturally for the majority of women. While the average American woman weighs 140 pounds (64 kg) and is five feet four inches tall (1.6 m), the average American model weighs 117 pounds (53 kg) and is five feet eleven inches (1.8 m).[3] The standard of beauty is high even for supermodels, who often aren't considered beautiful enough as-is.

LASHES DO LIE

Beauty standards are becoming impossible to achieve, even in advertisements. In 2017, in a mascara advertisement for the cosmetics company Rimmel, fashion model Cara Delevingne wore false eyelashes. She also had her lashes extended digitally in postproduction to look longer and more uniform, prompting the Advertising Standards Authority in the United Kingdom to ban the ad for being misleading.

Rimmel is not the only brand to mislead its consumers. In the last ten years, almost every major brand of mascara has had to either pull ads or settle lawsuits for false advertising. In 2011, Taylor Swift's ads promoting a CoverGirl mascara were discontinued when it was revealed after the shoot that Swift's eyelashes had been digitally enhanced to make them more dramatic in the advertisement. Natalie Portman's Dior mascara ad was pulled in the United Kingdom for the same reason in 2010.

Unfortunately, these pulled ads are the exception and not the rule. For every banned ad, thousands of other false images remain.

Models are hired to sell products. Cosmetic surgery, good lighting, expert makeup application, tailored clothing, and digital manipulation all combine to create an idea of the perfect woman that only exists in photographs. However, impossible beauty standards do not stop girls and women from chasing perfection at a young age. Studies show that children as young as five years old express dissatisfaction with their bodies because of media influence. Most girls compare themselves to fashion models and admit that pictures of models influence their idea of the ideal body, which in turn can cause lower levels of self-esteem. Not only do media images make women upset over their appearance, but they can cause feelings of anxiety and anger.

Media influence isn't limited to seeing celebrities. The amount of time a girl spends looking at social media images plays a large role in determining her level of self-esteem. These actions are associated with disordered eating and negative body image. Since the average teen spends almost 11 hours each day looking at various forms of media, there are plenty of opportunities for negativity to infiltrate her brain.[4]

In a world where women are constantly bombarded with unrealistic photographs, cultivating and maintaining high levels of self-esteem and positive body images is difficult but not impossible. It requires girls to stop listening to the lies presented in the media about beauty and women's bodies. Women can also start deprogramming years of internalized negativity. They can learn to appreciate their bodies the way they are. And the earlier a girl starts the process of improving her self-esteem, the better. Studies show that a girl's level of self-esteem starts to plummet around puberty, when her body shape begins to change, and then hits rock bottom around age 15. A girl's self-esteem does not begin to improve until around age 20.[5]

THE WHITENESS OF BEAUTY

While beauty standards are unattainable for nearly every woman, they are especially complicated for African-American, Asian, Hispanic, and Native American women. Although approximately one-third of people in the United States are people of color, this diversity is not fairly represented in advertisements, on fashion runways, or in commercial media images, where up to 88 percent of faces are white.[8] African-American women have been especially affected by white beauty standards. Audrey Elisa Kerr, a professor of African-American literature, is the author of *The Paper Bag Principle*. Her book explores how African-American men and women used to judge a person's beauty and value by whether his or her skin was lighter or darker than a paper bag. While actual paper bags are no longer used, white skin remains the stereotypical beauty ideal. Even when a woman of color is included in advertising today, the model often has a complexion and hair type that is closer to the white standard of beauty.

THE F-WORD: FAT

When it comes to body image, weight begins to press heaviest on the minds of girls at a very early age. More than 80 percent of ten-year-old girls are worried they might become fat.[6] Hoping to control their weight, one-half of teenage girls use unhealthy behaviors such as skipping meals, vomiting, fasting, smoking cigarettes, and taking laxatives.[7] However, statistics show girls who use unhealthy weight-control behaviors to stave off obesity have a higher body mass index (BMI) five years later than girls who do not engage in unhealthy dieting practices.

Teen girls who try to take care of and protect their bodies often find themselves accidentally steered towards disordered eating and exercise behaviors. This is thanks to a boom in online industries focused on selling beauty and wellness products that actually make many girls unwell.

Girls tend to know that "thinspiration" websites support eating disorders and should be avoided. But a new breed of "fitspiration" website has emerged. These websites appear, at first, to be a positive influence as girls work toward a healthy and fit lifestyle. However, a recent comparison of the two types of sites found that both contained the same hazardous messaging. Both praise thinness as the ultimate goal, criticizing fat, approving the objectification of the bodies of girls and women, and creating guilt about food and girls' bodies. It has become dangerously normalized and acceptable for girls to hate their bodies, even as they attempt to take care of themselves. This has created a lose-lose scenario that will take proactive work on the part of not just girls but also society at large to untangle self-worth from physical appearance, especially on social media.

HYPERSEXUALITY AND SELF-ESTEEM

Sex appeal is also intertwined in girls' self-esteem and body image. "There is so much pressure on teen girls and young women to portray themselves as sexy," says psychology professor Elizabeth Daniels, who studies the

Hating their bodies may cause some girls to develop eating disorders.

media's effect on girls' body images.[9] One effect modern media has had on young girls is hypersexualization. This is the acceptance and expectation of young girls and teens engaging in sexy actions and behaviors once typically reserved for adult women.

Hypersexuality encourages society to see girls and women as objects of desire first and puts the importance of sexual appeal above all other characteristics. Toddler girls are learning how to twerk, tween girls wear thong underwear to avoid panty lines, and teenagers wear heavy makeup and tight clothing to look like their favorite celebrities. Because sexual images are everywhere, hypersexuality has become a seemingly natural part of girls' lives.

When intelligence and creativity are less valued than appearance and sexiness, girls' self-esteem suffers, especially considering the double standards for girls and women. Hypersexualization of girls is especially threatening to their self-esteem. Instead of body image serving as a self-rating of physical appearance, sexualized media influences girls to focus on using their sexiness to attract others. "Why is it we focus so heavily on girls' appearances?" Daniels asks. "What does this tell us about gender?"[10] Teen girls are simultaneously encouraged to look sexy but not behave provocatively, to be attractive but

Many girls ignore sexist remarks made toward them.

not sexual. Because girls are so used to trying to attract male attention, some girls do not feel like they deserve to speak up against microaggressions from boys and men who catcall and make sexual advances. Many girls tend to swallow their embarrassment in these situations until it turns into shame and self-loathing.

Girls can work to cultivate an identity that has little or nothing to do with physical beauty. This can help girls avoid being obsessed with attractiveness. Recognizing when society treats women like objects and not people, as well as having the confidence to complain about microaggressions, is also empowering and productive. "Don't focus so heavily on appearance," Daniels encourages young women. "Focus on who you are as a person and what you do in the world."[11]

DISCUSSION STARTERS

- Do you agree with the study that found viewing images on social media can have a negative impact on a girl's self-esteem? Why or why not?
- If a teen girl tries to attract male attention, is it always a sign of low self-esteem? Explain your reasoning.

CHAPTER FOUR

GENDER-BASED VIOLENCE

In Massachusetts, a high school girl is stalked through her Twitter account by a boy from her church who wants to go out with her. He ignores her refusals and becomes increasingly demanding because he feels that she should give him a chance. In Oregon, a girl's mother threatens to kill her if she doesn't stop "being a lesbian." In Tennessee, the girls at one middle school often pretend to be sick at the end of the week to avoid "Bra Flick Fridays," when boys compete to flick as many bra straps as possible before the weekend begins. While these cases are hypothetical, they illustrate common experiences that girls face in the United States, and they are all examples of gender-based violence (GBV).

Anyone can perpetuate GBV.

GBV describes situations in which a woman or girl is targeted for physical, sexual, or psychological abuse or harassment specifically because she is female. A person's sexuality, ethnicity, class, and behaviors that do not fit local gender norms can increase the likelihood of GBV.

Boys can be victims of GBV as well. For example, they can be told to bottle up their emotions or take a punch like a man. But societal power imbalances cause girls to experience higher levels of sexual violence, harassment, psychological bullying, and cyberbullying. Imbalances happen when the opinions and actions of one group have more respect and power than those of another.

For example, while a school's student body might be 50 percent female and 50 percent male, if there is a power imbalance, and the school administration has not created a culture in which male students are expected to respect female students, "Bra Flick Fridays" can go unreported or

LGBTQ BULLYING

Lesbian, gay, bisexual, transgender, and queer (LGBTQ) students face much higher rates of harassment and bullying than straight students. Nearly 60 percent of LGBTQ students reported feeling unsafe at school.[1] One-third of lesbian, gay, and bisexual students report being bullied at school.[2] For transgender students, bullying, harassment, and assault can be even more damaging. Approximately 41 percent of transgender Americans attempt suicide, compared to the under 5 percent of the overall population in America who attempt suicide.[3]

SCHOOL SHOULD BE A SAFE SPACE

Despite laws that are supposed to prevent GBV, it is still common in schools in the United States. All public schools and private schools that receive federal funding are legally mandated to provide a safe and equal environment for girls to learn. The law that mandates this, Title IX, was passed in 1972 and was designed to eliminate gender inequity in schools, most notably around education, athletics, and GBV.

But some schools still do not follow all of the rules. This creates unhealthy educational environments where girls do not have a safe learning space. Legally, if a student is a victim of GBV by a fellow student, teacher, or school employee, and she or her guardian puts in a complaint to the school, the school must not only investigate the concern immediately but also develop a safety plan to keep the girl safe from verbal or physical retaliation. It is illegal for a girl to be forced to work things out or have any direct contact with an alleged attacker.

ignored if reported. And the only people who are punished for the boys' actions are the girls upon whom the harassment is inflicted.

GBV is not limited to school. Approximately 85 percent of American girls are harassed on the street before they are 17 years old.[4] Street harassment can be verbal, such as catcalling or whistling, and it often escalates. One-half of women under the age of 40 report being fondled or groped by strangers.[5] GBV is prevalent in US homes as well. It can be seen through physical or sexual violence, and in more subtle psychological ways, such as when a girl is told by a parent that she is worthless if she loses her virginity. The latter is psychological GBV because the message is different for boys, who are often praised in American culture for sexual prowess.

However, power imbalances are not necessarily permanent. School-related GBV is less common for high school seniors than for freshmen. Educating people on what is and is not acceptable behavior can greatly reduce instances of GBV and also empower victims to stand up for their right to feel safe in their environments. The cost of inaction and avoidance of the topic is severe. GBV victims suffer low levels of self-esteem and higher rates of depression, which affect life choices and an individual's potential for greatness.

In a perfect world, girls and boys would instantly have equal levels of authority and respect in society, and there would be no violence toward a person on the basis of gender. Although the United States is working toward this goal, equality can appear as the exception rather than the rule.

PHYSICAL AND SEXUAL GBV

One in four girls is sexually abused before age 18.[6] Approximately 42 percent of girls were physically assaulted at least once in the past 12 months.[7] Until rather recently in US history it was difficult to convince society to consider physical and sexual violence against women and girls as wrong because by law, girls and women were considered the property of men.

Legally, the bodies of both girls and boys are still seen as property in the United States. It is legal for a parent to hit a child in all 50 states and the District of Columbia. Nineteen states still allow children to be spanked or physically punished at school. Allowing adults to hit children affects GBV. When violence of any sort is condoned, it normalizes other types of violence, fails to hold the perpetrator accountable for his or her harmful actions, and shames victims into not speaking up, either in fear of repercussions or because the victims believe they deserve the violence.

When a person's body is violated, no matter how small or large the infraction, it chips away at self-esteem and normalizes violence. This paves the way for escalated instances of GBV. For example, if a girl is given a swat on the behind in class for misbehaving, a boy who sees this might decide to casually slap her on her bottom in the hallway. He is emboldened to act this way because the school has made it clear the girl's body is eligible to be violated. The girl might think it is easier to ignore the boy than complain. She might be told that her misbehaving caused the situation by drawing attention to herself. Or she might be told that boys will be boys. Then, feeding off of the inaction of the girl, the boy could be encouraged to progress his assault with groping. This power imbalance, in which the girl does not feel protected by or safe in her environment, is part of what leads 10 percent of teen girls to be physically forced into unwanted sexual intercourse.[8]

A woman's right to physical and sexual safety even in her own household has gone unprotected for most of US history. The first rape laws were similar to property laws in that they were put in place to benefit men, who were considered to be women's owners. Men did not want their wives sullied or their daughters' virginities taken mainly because it lowered their value. As late as the 1990s, US laws often protected a man's right to inflict violence upon

BROCK TURNER: POWER MEETS INJUSTICE

Most sexual assaults go unreported, but even when victims speak up, justice is often not served. In 2015, Stanford University student Brock Turner sexually assaulted an unconscious woman in front of multiple witnesses, who testified against him in court. Turner was convicted by a unanimous jury of sexually penetrating an unconscious person and assault with intent to commit rape. Even with the evidence and conviction, the judge sentenced Turner, who was a star athlete, to only six months in jail, saying that "a prison sentence would have a severe impact on him." During the trial, Turner's father begged for leniency because he suggested a 15-year sentence was "a steep price to pay for 20 minutes of action out of his 20 years of life."[9] He also expressed sadness that his son no longer wanted to eat steak, his favorite food, because of his actions.

Turner was released from jail after three months. Many people were outraged at his mild punishment. They believed the judge had put Turner's comfort and future over justice for the victim.

Brock Turner engaged in sexual GBV when he assaulted a woman behind a dumpster in 2015.

women in his own family. In 1910, the US Supreme
Court said that a wife beaten by her husband had no
legal recourse. In 1992, a husband in North Carolina or
Oklahoma could still rape his wife without fear of being
arrested. These two states were the last to pass legislation
requiring the courts to allow a woman the ability to refuse
sex with her husband and the right to press charges if her
body was violated. Legal recognition of rape as a crime
against the victim herself was a major women's rights
milestone. It legitimized a woman's ownership of her
own body.

PSYCHOLOGICAL GBV

People often think of violent actions as the kind that
leave physical marks, but GBV can also be psychological,
expressed as verbal and emotional abuse. Adults and
peers alike can be the source of psychological GBV. For
example, in the hallway students might yell after a girl
they don't like, "You're a dumb slut." A mother might
take a cookie out of her daughter's mouth because "no
one likes a fat girl." A romantic partner might threaten
to post pictures he took of a girl naked unless she stops
complaining about his attitude.

Because there are no physical marks, it is often
difficult to pinpoint and track psychological abuse, but the

SIGNS OF AN ABUSIVE RELATIONSHIP

Girls and women under the age of 24 suffer the highest rate of dating violence.[11] But only approximately half of teenage girls between the ages of 11 and 14 say they know how to identify the warning signs.[12] Common red flags in a partner's behavior include an exploding temper, erratic mood swings, possessive behavior, checking the other person's cell phones, e-mails or social networks without permission, and repeatedly pressuring the other person to have sex.

repercussions of cyberbullying, teasing, screaming, and name-calling are long-lasting for the victim. Research has shown that psychological abuse in childhood is just as damaging as sexual or physical abuse, and it is strongly associated with anxiety, depression, and low self-esteem.

Approximately 93 percent of girls who are sexually assaulted are related to or otherwise know the assailant.[10] Gender expectations and power imbalances within relationships often complicate justice and fairness when it comes to punishment for the assaulter and support for the victim. Assaulters sometimes do not see anything wrong with their actions and blame the victim or otherwise dismiss her concerns. For example, parents guilty of psychological GBV might say their verbal abuse stems from how much they care about the girl. A romantic partner might blame a girl's attractiveness for his sexual assault. The latter is an example of dating violence, which is a significant issue for teens. One in five teenage girls suffers physical or sexual abuse from a person she is dating.[13]

Because sexual and physical violence is so pervasive in the United States, it is taking a long time for culture to catch up with the law. Tremendous effort is needed to shift gender norms so microaggressions such as bottom-slapping are no longer categorized as boys being boys, and larger acts of violence such as rape are not blamed on the victim because of her clothing. A new generation of male and female leaders, starting in middle and high school, need to speak out and use their voices to create change in their own communities to end violence against women.

DISCUSSION STARTERS

- Have you been in a situation where the power imbalance between a man and a woman is especially apparent? What are some ways that you might have been able to bring about equality in the situation?
- Why do you believe sexual assault is common in our society?
- What do you think needs to change in order for GBV to stop?

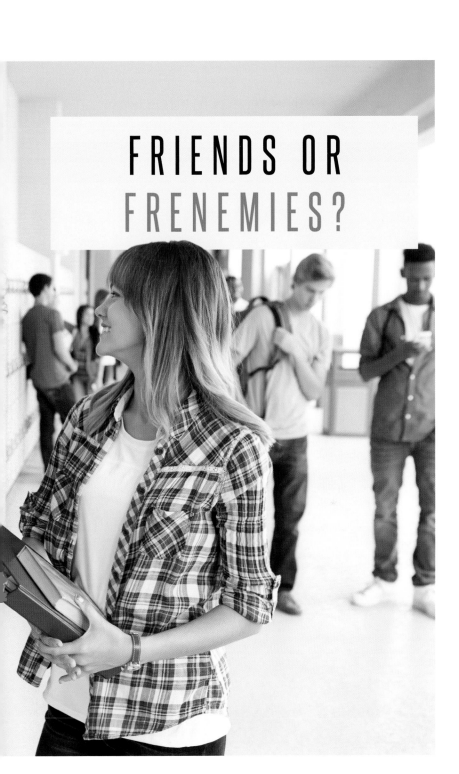

CHAPTER FIVE

FRIENDS OR FRENEMIES?

A girl tends to have three types of friends in her social circle: a best friend, close friends, and acquaintances. But studies show there's almost no such thing as forever when it comes to friends. By twelfth grade, 99 percent of girls who were friends in seventh grade are no longer

Friends that girls make in elementary school will not necessarily be their friends as they grow up.

friends.[1] It is natural to switch friend groups multiple times over the years. As people evolve and change, so do their relationships. The media, however, does not present this reality accurately.

Rachel Simmons is a leadership development specialist at Smith College. She has studied friendship patterns in teen girls and believes "girls receive unrealistic messages about how to have a friendship."[2] According to Simmons, the media portrays female friendships inaccurately, showing a group of girls as either a "bestie love-fest" where nobody ever fights, or a "mean girl-fest" where nobody is ever nice.[3] Neither of these types of friendships are healthy or realistic. Simmons believes that because girls aren't prepared for the reality of authentic friendships, which all come with

FRIEND DIVORCE

Friendships are not always destined to be lifelong. The hermit crab and its shell may be a good analogy for healthy relationships. As a hermit crab grows, it must move to different shells that better fit its expanding body. It sheds its old shell and scoots off to find a new one that feels better, which another crab has left behind. Soon, another hermit crab happily climbs into the shell that it leaves. This cycle continues for years. There is nothing wrong with the old shells, or the old friendships, other than the fact that they simply no longer fit.

It can be painful as a girl finds herself coming to the end of a close friendship. Leadership specialist Rachel Simmons believes teen girls should honor their emotions and refer to these breakups as friend divorces, saying, "Just like people date and break up, friends break up, too. Friend divorce is a sign that something was broken in your relationship, and it creates space in your life to let the next good friend in."[4]

conflict and ups and downs, they blame themselves for failing to carry a close friendship forever.

TOXIC FRIENDSHIPS

A healthy friendship is one in which two or more people trust, support, and uplift each other. An unhealthy, or toxic friendship, does the opposite and makes a person feel worse about herself and less certain of her abilities. Most girls will, at some point in their lives, find themselves in a toxic friendship.

Some toxic friendships are accidental. Amanda Rose, professor of psychology at the University of Missouri, says that one of the reasons a friend, even a best friend, might no longer be a good fit is a tendency of girls to obsessively discuss problems with their friends. Instead of inspiring or lifting each other up with positive discussions, many friends focus on the negative, constantly talking about problems and bad feelings without creating an active plan for improvement. There are positive elements to discussing issues with a friend, such as increasing closeness. But too much focus on problems with friends can cause increased levels of depression and contribute to lower levels of self-esteem.

Other toxic friendships are more problematic. Some common examples include a rumor-spreading frenemy who is always nice in person or a mean clique that forces one friend to change her habits because she is considered uncool. Often a girl might feel trapped in a toxic friendship for fear that the negativity she experiences will escalate to bullying if the friendship ends. While it may seem like a toxic friendship provides protection from isolation, in many ways being stuck in the toxicity can be worse.

ONLINE FRIENDS AND ENEMIES

More than one-half of teen girls have made a new friend online. This is a predictable statistic considering that the Internet is the third most popular place for teenagers to hang out, after "school" and "someone's house."[5] When not meeting new people

INCOME INEQUALITY AND SOCIAL ISOLATION

In a world where technology access factors into everyday life, not being able to afford electronics can be a blow to a teen's schoolwork and social life. While more than 85 percent of teenagers have access to a cell phone and a computer, for the 15 percent who do not, social isolation is a huge problem.[6]

Mary Brown is the executive director of the D.C. Promise Neighborhood Initiative. She sees the lack of technology in low-income homes as a "consistent lack of opportunity that really leads to this whole cycle of poverty."[7] When there is no computer or Internet at home, it is more difficult for a teen to research college scholarships or summer jobs. Without a cell phone, she is left out of bonding opportunities with friends. Even when kids aren't on their computers or phones they are often talking about what happened while they were using them, further isolating the teen without these items. The same issue comes up with extracurricular activities. Teens who do not have reliable transportation or money to cover fees often are unable to participate in activities.

on social media, most teens are spending time online with their real-life friends, too. Nearly one-half of teens feel pressure to only post content that puts them in a positive light and avoid sharing real-life drama.[8] This pressure comes from not only wanting to look cool and successful but also from a need for attention. More than one-third of teens say they feel pressure to only post content that will get lots of likes and comments.[9] Fortunately, most teenagers realize the lives people present on social media aren't the full story, but it does not completely eliminate the instinct to compare their lives to another's. Many girls digitally alter their photos to present a particular image of themselves on social media. While most teen users have positive things to say about social media and how it affects their friendships, one out of every five teen social media users say that seeing what other people post on social media makes them feel worse about their own life.[10]

The more time a girl spends online, the more open she is to cyberbullying. Statistics show that 87 percent of teens have witnessed cyberbullying online.[11] While boys are more likely to be involved in physical bullying than girls, girls are more likely to both experience cyberbullying and to be a cyberbully.

Cyberbullying can feel more intense and vicious than in-person bullying. In real life, a person can get away from

Cell phones have become another tool for bullies to use against their victims.

SERIOUS CYBERBULLYING CONSEQUENCES

Cyberbullying is linked to a higher rate of suicide attempts. The increase in cyberbullying during the past decade and its growing impact has led it to be labeled a serious crime in many states. Teens who cyberbully are being arrested for their actions. In 2016, in Waukesha, Wisconsin, police worked with the school district to arrest an 11-year-old fourth grader for anonymously cyberbullying students using a school-issued iPad. In 2017, the abusers of an 18-year-old Texas girl who killed herself after months of cyberbullying were arrested and charged. And in 2013, two sixth-grade girls were arrested for cyberbullying a 12-year-old girl who committed suicide.

a bully. But online it is easy to feel as if the bully is always there unless the social media account is deleted, an act that can further isolate the victim.

Psychologist Susan Swearer is the cofounder of the Bullying Research Network. "People are more likely to write horrible things when they think they're being anonymous," she points out.[12] While the cyberbully is trying to make the victim believe something is wrong with her, Swearer says it's actually the cyberbully with the problem. "From a psychological perspective, people who write horrible things about other people . . . have their own mental health issues."[13] While multiple states across the country have made cyberbullying a crime, it is still as commonplace as ever. Many bullies think they're having harmless fun behind a phone or a computer screen, but the truth is that cyberbullying is as damaging as in-person bullying. Cyberbullying has been linked to numerous acts of self-harm across the United States.

As painful as it may be, a cyberbully victim should keep copies and screenshots of any threats made online, especially if the cyberbully attends her school. Many schools are starting to incorporate cyberbullying into school anti-bullying policies, even if the cyberbullying happens away from school. No one online has the right to harass or make an individual feel unsafe.

DISCUSSION STARTERS

- Both cyberbullying and in-person bullying are harmful to the victim's health. How are these two types of bullying the same? How are they different?

- Which do you believe is worse: having no friends or having toxic friends? Support your answer.

- Have you ever cyberbullied anyone, or have you been the victim of cyberbullying? What can you do to stop cyberbullying?

CHAPTER SIX

NOT ALL GIRLS ARE PRO-GIRL

A person doesn't have to be male to have prejudice or to discriminate against females. In fact, one of the key factors undermining progress towards gender equality is ingrained sexism. From birth, a girl is bombarded with sexist gender norms and misogynistic stereotypes about a female's place and her rights. In 2016, eight-year-old Daisy Edmonds had her YouTube video go viral after she ranted about how shirt designs for boys encouraged imagination, while shirts for girls emphasized beauty. That same year, a woman's Facebook post drew outrage after she compared the popular magazines *Girls' Life* and *Boys' Life*. The *Boys' Life* cover focused on exploring future careers, while the one for girls focused on hair and fashion.

A girl's identity is often tied up in impossible beauty standards, GBV, and sexist practices and beliefs prevalent in her community. Because sexism and misogyny are ingrained in American society, they're

MISOGYNY VS. SEXISM

While many people use the terms *sexism* and *misogyny* interchangeably, they are slightly different. Feminist scholar Naomi Wolf, author of *The Beauty Myth*, describes a sexist person as someone who might "like women quite a lot in person but be very happy to support systematic discrimination against them."[1] On the other hand, someone who is misogynistic dislikes women and feels hatred toward them. Such a person often wants to hurt a woman who stands up for herself either physically or emotionally. While not all sexists are misogynists, misogynists are typically sexist.

impossible to avoid. Most girls and women work hard to conform to societal standards to avoid being ostracized or bullied. Somewhere along the way, these beliefs become attached to a girl's sense of self. The beliefs are incorrectly categorized as biological facts or as an unchangeable part of culture. But evenually, many so-called biological facts are debunked as opinions, including the notions that girls do not have the common sense to choose their own marriage partners and that female bodies are too fragile to play sports.

As feminists and activists fought for these old ideas to become obsolete myths, some women had no interest in changing the social norms. Today, remaining ingrained cultural beliefs cause some girls and women to doubt whether they are deserving of equality. "Women who internalize sexism are more likely

PORTRAIT OF ANTI-SUFFRAGISTS

Throughout history, as many American women fought for gender equality, there have always been a number of women who fought against advancement for women because they wanted to keep things as they were. The right to vote was one such dividing issue. Suffragettes fought the uphill battle for more than a century to achieve women's voting rights. But anti-suffragists did not believe women should vote. These women tended to support gender norms and "were generally women of wealth, privilege, social status and even political power," says Corrine McConnaughy, a political science professor at George Washington University. "They were women who were doing, comparatively, quite well under the existing system, with incentives to hang onto a system that privileged them."[2]

Women face pressure to conform to social norms, including the pressure to follow specific standards of beauty.

to diet, to be critical of their appearance if they don't meet the impossible appearance standards that we see in the media, but likewise it can make women judge other women along those same lines," says Kjerstin Gruys, a sociology professor at the University of Nevada, Reno.[3]

For example, because US gender norms state that body hair on women should be removed, some women insult those who choose not to shave. In addition, if a woman proposes to her boyfriend or a teen girl invites a boy to prom, internalized sexism can lead to gossip about the woman or girl's pushiness and desperation.

Admitting that some societal norms are misguided and unfair might be difficult for, and cause resentment in, women who adhere to the rules. This is because this admission suggests their identity and core beliefs are flawed. An attack on gender norms can at first feel like a personal attack.

THE "OTHER GIRLS" MYTH

One way society causes girls to undermine each other and perpetuate negative gender stereotypes is by encouraging girls to buy into the "other girls" myth. The myth suggests that there are some girls who believe they shouldn't be grouped with the rest. These girls claim they are superior to others because they don't act like stereotypical girls. One example of this myth is heard in singer-songwriter Taylor Swift's song, "You Belong With Me." In this song, Swift sings about how a boy should date her instead of the cheer captain. Swift claims to be different from this girl because Swift wears sneakers and T-shirts and likes to watch sports. The other girl, Swift claims, meets female stereotypes and is superficial.

One way this myth is perpetuated is by complimenting a girl on how unique she is as compared to others. Talia Baurer is a writer and advocate who has explored internalized sexism in her own life. Baurer writes that when a compliment compares or contrasts a woman to

WONDER WOMAN

One way that some girls do not support other girls is by taking stereotypes at face value, often by accident. For example, the 2017 *Wonder Woman* film was considered to be a major milestone for the representation of women on-screen in powerful roles. But the main black female character was essentially Wonder Woman's nanny. This stereotypical role does not increase the public perception of black women as multifaceted people.

other women, such as "you're so different from other women," this statement is not a compliment but is actually insulting and "reinforces the dynamic that women must compete with each other for male attention and approval."[4]

The intersection of class, race, and sexuality also leads to different types of othering. "We've all been taught to believe degrading stereotypes about people based on their race, age, ability, size, class, gender identity, gender expression, sexuality, and myriad other identities," Baurer continues. "And no matter how hard we work to unlearn that, it's hard to shake."[5]

Some girls who want to fit in and fear isolation tear down others to improve their social standing. For example, in the United States girls often bully girls who they believe are too sexually permissive, or promiscuous. Leora Tanenbaum is the author of *Slut! Growing Up Female with a Bad Reputation*. In her research she found that contradicting messages about how girls should behave sexually are confusing and stressful, so "the way they deal with their anxiety is pointing their fingers at other girls."[6] Nearly all of the girls she interviewed were called "sluts," not by males but by other girls. "Girls wouldn't feel the need to do this if we had one sexual standard," Tanenbaum

INGRAINED SEXISM STARTS EARLY

A recent Harvard study of thousands of 11- to 18-year-old girls and boys in the United States found that stereotypical gender assumptions about who makes the best leaders are locked in at an early age. Forty percent of boys said they preferred male political leaders to female ones. Additionally, only 8 percent of girls said they preferred female political leaders.[9] This internalized sexism over gender roles stayed with the students into their own school elections. When students were asked to support various leadership scenarios, they were most likely to support student councils led by white boys, and least likely to support councils led by white girls. One main reason for this gap is that white girls tended to not support other white girls seeking power.

said. "It's because we have the double standard that this phenomenon occurs."[7]

COMRADE OR COMPETITION?

A large factor in the continuation of the "other girls" myth is the false belief that women and girls naturally see each other as competition, while men naturally see other men as equals. Sheryl Sandberg, the chief operating officer of Facebook, said, "The biggest enemy of women, we're warned, is a powerful woman." But statistically, she continues, "women aren't any meaner to women than men are to one another. Women are just expected to be nicer. We stereotype men as aggressive and women as kind. When women violate those stereotypes, we judge them harshly."[8]

Sandberg believes unhealthy female relationships can be stopped if people stop judging a behavior more

Instead of viewing other girls as competition, girls can learn to support one another and foster positive relationships.

Sheryl Sandberg believes it's important to teach girls how to be leaders from a young age.

harshly when it comes from a woman rather than a man. "Women can disagree—even compete—and still have one another's backs," Sandberg says.[10] Then, Sandberg believes, the "other girls" myth and the notion that women are not comrades but competitors will fade over time.

Through awareness, activism, and female mentoring, it is expected that more girls and women will take on leadership roles and create healthier environments for all people to succeed. "When a woman helps another woman, they both benefit," Sandberg says. "And when women celebrate one another's accomplishments, we're all lifted up."[11]

DISCUSSION STARTERS

- Do you believe you've ever said something sexist to a girl? What might you do differently if you were in that situation today?
- What are some examples of the "other girls" myth that you've seen in the media?
- Do you think girls and women are judged more harshly than boys and men? Why or why not?

CHAPTER SEVEN

YOU'RE PRETTIER
WHEN YOU SMILE

By middle school, some girls wake up every morning knowing to expect uninvited comments about their appearance throughout the day. On the school bus, a friend might tell a girl that her shirt makes her look thinner than usual. Or while the girl is laughing at a joke, a teacher might say that she's so much prettier when she smiles. At lunch, a boy might look at the girl's skirt and yell out in front of the entire cafeteria, "Great legs!" But none of these expressions are compliments.

These situations are not uplifting to the girl. Saying she looks thinner reflects the fact that the speaker does not think the girl's body is good enough most days. Suggesting a girl is prettier when she smiles encourages her to act happy all of the time for the benefit and approval of others. Yelling about a girl's body across a room objectifies the girl.

Lauren Greenfield is an award-winning documentarian who directed the viral #LikeAGirl ad campaign that worked to expose stereotypes regarding the strength and abilities of girls and young women. Her conversations with teen girls and research into the topic led her to realize that "the compliments we so frequently and often unconsciously bestow on girls can actually have a negative effect and even become a source of pain and

Lauren Greenfield received an Emmy Award for her LikeAGirl commercial.

disempowerment." Even properly polite compliments about a girl's appearance can cause more harm than good. Greenfield explains that compliments "related to physical appearance like 'you're so cute' . . . were perceived as limiting and oppressive, making girls feel that the expectations on them were focused on their appearance and not on their abilities or what was inside."[1]

Appearance praise is not only limiting because of the message, but also because it is often the only type of compliment a girl receives. Telling a girl she is pretty might make her feel good in the moment, but it redirects the girl's energy to her appearance over other more permanent aspects of herself. From an early age, "girls are complimented on their appearance and the focus stays on appearance," says Tricia

FLIP THE GENDER SCRIPT

Pushback is common when confronting people about sexist statements. It's difficult for some people to understand that what they see as a friendly interaction could be perceived otherwise. So in these situations, many people can become defensive. Still, in a safe environment, it is best to tell the commenters that their comments are inappropriate and should stop. If the reaction is negative, instead of letting the conversation devolve into a shouting match, flip the gender script. Ask the person if he or she would say to a man the same thing that caused concern. If not, explain that is why the words were sexist. Even if the person's comment was not made with the intent to be discriminatory or hurtful, it can still be the result of ingrained or subconscious sexism the person should be made aware of. After all, if a guy wouldn't tell Ben that he looks prettier when he smiles, then he shouldn't say it to Jen.

Berry, director of the Women in Engineering Program at the University of Texas. "Kids pick up on these things at early ages and internalize what is important and how they are valued."[2]

For decades, social scientists have studied gender bias in teacher-student interactions. They've found that teachers frequently do not treat girls and boys the same, although they believe that they do. Boys receive more overall attention in the classroom. And when teachers praise girls, it is often about their physical appearance or the neatness of their work. Boys, however, are praised for their ability to accomplish a task or solve a problem.

Many of these interactions have been socially acceptable for generations and are only now becoming outdated. While it is taking a long time for awareness of these biases and how they affect girls to permeate, progress is being made. The issue of complicated compliments is old news. What is new is the large number of people who are actively trying to change the way people talk about girls and women. Many teachers guilty of sexist communication will change their behaviors once they learn they are harming their students.

Compliments can be positive and healthy.

NO, YOU'RE THE SMARTEST!

Separating damaging appearance-based compliments from positive ones about people's abilities is a battle. Learning how to accept praise is another difficult

challenge. When a compliment is given, the recipient has
the option of accepting, rejecting, or deflecting. Some
girls and women tend to reject outright or deflect praise
instead of accepting a compliment. "[We're told] love

yourself, but not too much. Be confident, but practice
a style of humility this culture never requires of men.
Believe in yourself, but never admit it out loud, lest you
make another woman who doesn't feel good about herself
feel bad," says Renee Engeln, a psychology professor at
Northwestern University.[3]

Self-esteem levels have little to do with being able to
accept a compliment. Social psychologist Laura Brannon
suggests women with high self-esteem reject compliments
to seem modest, while those with low self-esteem reject
them because they don't believe them. Engeln adds, "If
you're raised to think it's arrogant to ever say something
positive about yourself, it makes it hard to accept a
compliment."[4] Some experts suggest that thinking of a
good compliment as a gift makes it easier to accept.

ADDICTED TO PRAISE

Conversely, some teen girls find themselves addicted to
praise. Praise addiction can result in a growing tolerance
to compliments. Over time, individual compliments and
praise lose value so that more are needed to feel normal.

Praise addictions aren't easy to beat, either. Martha
Beck, an author who has written about praise addiction
and interviewed praise-addicted teen girls, noted, "Like
food addiction, praise addiction is complex because it's

impossible to simply eliminate your drug of choice. Some amount of narcissistic supply is normal and healthy (and people probably won't stop giving compliments)."[5]

Peggy Klaus, the author of *The Hard Truth about Soft Skills*, said praise junkies need to learn how to "feel good from the inside. You have to build up your own reserves of self-esteem." Klaus adds that growing up a girl in the United States can make it difficult to have high levels of self-esteem without external validation, but it is not impossible. Girls can learn to give themselves credit, Klaus continues, instead of "looking to others to give [them] the confidence, the self-esteem, the self-respect."[6]

DISCUSSION STARTERS

- Do you think it's okay for a person to give an unsolicited comment about a girl's physical appearance? Why or why not? Are there exceptions to your belief?
- How do you feel when someone gives you a compliment? How do you respond, and why do you think that is the case?
- In your own words, what's the difference between a girl feeling good from the inside verses needing compliments to feel good?

TODAY'S GIRLS,
TOMORROW'S
WOMEN

When Kaitlyn Juvik started her Facebook page "No Bra, No Problem" to tell the world about her school's reaction to girls going braless, she had no idea that her experience would resonate with so many other girls and women. Today, the Facebook page has thousands of followers. Thousands of girls and women around the world have tweeted braless photos of themselves using the hashtag #NoBraNoProblem. However, Kaitlyn's accidental activism has not been an entirely positive experience, as she has faced online harassment from people around the world. "I've had a lot of awful comments. I've been called every name in the book. People have sent me messages saying 'kill yourself,' [and] 'you're a huge whore,'" she said.[1]

It's not unusual for people to try to shut down women who speak up for themselves. But Kaitlyn had the confidence to stand her ground. She showcased the importance of women and girls standing up for themselves on issues big and small.

Social media is a powerful tool that people are using to start conversations about social issues.

"I'm extremely thankful that the word has gotten out. But I don't want the focus to be on the bra anymore," Kaitlyn says. "It started with me, but it's not about me. It's about women everywhere being able to be comfortable in their own bodies."[2]

CONFIDENCE IS EARNED, NOT GIVEN

Most girls have experiences that slowly chip away at their confidence levels over the years. Because of this, when thrust into a situation where something feels wrong, it can be difficult for girls and women to admit that they deserve better and scary to fight for what is right.

Fortunately, there is an unlimited supply of confidence in the world; it is just up to young women to grab it. Mindy Kaling is an Indian-American actress and best-selling author who has opened up about her confidence struggles over the years. She says that one of the most important lessons she learned is that "confidence is like respect; you have to earn it."[3] Just like a person can't just jump into the pool and become an Olympic swimmer in a few days, confidence takes years of time and effort to build up.

Katie Orenstein is the founder and director of the OpEd Project, where she empowers women to submit opinion pieces to newspapers to influence public policy.

Mindy Kaling strives to be a role model for girls.

GIRL, BOY, OR PURPLE PENGUIN?

Many schools around the country are trying to address biases that detract from the equal education of girls and boys. Some are creating more gender-neutral environments that are welcoming and inclusive of young people from all walks of life. For example, instead of separating children in the traditional girls' and boys' lines, inclusive schools use traits unrelated to gender, such as odd and even birth dates. The transition, although it typically receives positive feedback from students, is not always easy or accepted. In 2014, a Nebraska school district made national headlines when it encouraged classroom gender inclusivity by suggesting teachers refer to students not as girls and boys but as something gender neutral. The school superintendent suggested purple penguins as a possibility, a label considered absurd by many who did not understand the goal of the effort, which was to offer students labels that did not carry any ingrained gender norms.

Surprised to realize that 85 percent of opinion pieces were written by men, Orenstein recognized that many women might need a confidence boost to realize their opinions mattered and were desperately needed for equality's sake.[4]

Confidence is a crucial part of the future of young women and girls in the United States, because not only is confidence earned, it is also taught. Women's confidence is frequently undermined by gender norms and stereotypes in the United States. New generations of female-friendly leaders can flip this and teach girls to believe in themselves, not stereotypes.

A recent study of six-year-olds found that after entering school, where gender norms are confirmed and validated, girls start to believe boys are more likely to be brilliant and more capable of "really, really smart" activities than girls are.[5] School, media, peers, teachers,

Ignoring gender stereotypes in the classroom can help students succeed.

MISSING HIGH SCHOOL STEM GIRLS

While girls and women are entering science, technology, engineering, and math (STEM) fields, the numbers still need improvement, especially in high school course enrollment. Male students are more likely to take engineering courses, but the biggest disparity is found in AP computer science course enrollment—81 percent male and only 19 percent female.[8]

and parents seem to "lead girls away from the types of activities that are for really smart kids," says psychologist Lin Bian, who conducted the research.[6] At school, girls have much more exposure to cultural messages and "learn a great deal of the information about the social world," Bian continues. These early messages keep girls from considering themselves brilliant, which poses a threat to their futures. When these confidence-stunted girls reach adulthood, convincing them otherwise will be very hard. Bian says, "We need to do something from early on."[7]

WHAT'S NEXT?

The modern-day world for girls is different than it was in the United States in the 1800s. Many girls today would not have been able to receive a formal education because it was viewed as neither a right nor a priority for most girls. Marriage and childbearing were the main focus for the majority of girls and women in the United States until barely more than a generation ago. While the past is the past, the future is entirely up to this generation's girls and boys. The future will be determined by the amount of effort they put into fighting for what they believe, in terms of passing laws, funding programs, and championing cultural beliefs that support gender equality. Old stereotypes and gender norms often remain in place far longer than necessary. The more American girls and women are heard in the classroom and the boardroom, and the more women run for political office, the faster the wheel will spin toward a future where every gender is equal.

DISCUSSION STARTERS

- Why do you think Kaitlyn and other gender-equality activists receive so many threatening messages?
- What are some topics on which you would like to have your voice heard? Name three ways you can achieve this goal.
- How would you like the social world of girls and women to change in the next 100 years? Can you think of any ways that you can help bring about this future?

ESSENTIAL FACTS

SIGNIFICANT EVENTS

- In the 1800s, women and men began advocating for economic, political, and social equality for both sexes. They became known as feminists.

- In 1920, the Nineteenth Amendment gave women the right to vote.

- The rise of social media allowed large numbers of people to quickly identify acts of sexism toward girls, sparking outrage and change in various situations.

KEY PLAYERS

- Kaitlyn Juvik began a movement that brought attention to how society sexualizes women's bodies through her social media page "No Bra, No Problem." The movement captured the attention of people around the world.

- Dr. Maria do Mar Pereira conducted research and found that educating students on how gender traits are formed decreases bullying based on gender stereotypes.

IMPACT ON SOCIETY

Before Title IX was passed in 1972, girls and women could be legally discriminated against and excluded from sports, clubs, and other educational opportunities in public schools and colleges. In the decades since its passage, girls have legally gained access to all opportunities that boys have, though inequity still exists in practice. Many organizations are working to fill in the gaps by boosting girls' confidence in their ability to play sports, code, and excel in STEM activities and participate in other activities usually reserved for men and boys.

QUOTE

"Sometimes adults think it's impossible to change gender norms because they're already so deeply entrenched. But they're much more entrenched in adults than they are in young people."

—*Dr. Maria do Mar Pereira, sociologist at the University of Warwick*

GLOSSARY

ACTIVISM
Working to bring about change.

CYBERBULLYING
The use of the Internet to bully or harass, including sending intimidating messages, posting unwanted photos and videos, or creating false profiles.

FEMINISM
The belief that women should have the same opportunities and rights as men politically, socially, and economically.

INGRAINED
Established; difficult to change.

INTERSECTIONALITY
Overlapping forms of oppression based on race, gender, class, sexuality, and other factors.

MISOGYNY

An attitude that looks down on women and girls.

PERPETRATOR

Someone who is responsible for an act.

SEXISM

Discrimination or prejudice toward people based on their sex.

STEREOTYPE

A widely held but oversimplified idea about a particular type of person or thing.

TRANSGENDER

A person whose gender identity, expression, or behavior is different from those typically associated with their assigned sex at birth.

ADDITIONAL
RESOURCES

SELECTED BIBLIOGRAPHY

American Civil Liberties Union. "Gender-Based Violence & Harassment: Your School, Your Rights." *VAWnet.* National Resource Center on Domestic Violence, n.d. Web. 5 June 2017.

Baumgardner, Jennifer. *F'em!.* Berkeley, CA: Seal, 2011. Print.

Paoletti, Jo B. *Pink and Blue: Telling the Boys from the Girls in America.* Bloomington, IN: Indiana UP, 2012. Print.

FURTHER READINGS

Bialik, Mayim. *Girling Up: How to Be Strong, Smart and Spectacular.* New York: Philomel, 2017. Print.

Kilpatrick, Haley. *The Drama Years: Real Girls Talk about Surviving Middle School–Bullies, Brands, Body Image, and More.* New York: Free Press, 2012. Print.

Taylor, Julia V. *The Body Image Workbook for Teens: Activities to Help Girls Develop a Healthy Body Image in an Image-Obsessed World.* Oakland, CA: New Harbinger, 2014. Print.

ONLINE RESOURCES

To learn more about growing up a girl, visit **abdobooklinks.com**. These links are routinely monitored and updated to provide the most current information available.

MORE INFORMATION

For more information on this subject, contact or visit the following organizations:

GIRLS FOR A CHANGE
PO Box 1436
San Jose, CA 95109
866-738-4422
girlsforachange.org

Girls for a Change is a nonprofit organization encouraging black girls and other girls of color to visualize their bright futures and potential.

GIRLS INC.
120 Wall Street
New York, NY 10005-3902
212-509-2000
girlsinc.org

Girls Inc. empowers and educates girls to break through the traditional barriers.

SOURCE NOTES

CHAPTER 1. DRESS CODE DRAMA

1. Chris Owsalt. "Alleged Dress-Code Violation Triggers Protest at Helena High School." *3KRTV*. KRTV.com, 28 May 2016. Web. 17 Aug. 2017.

2. Lily Puckett. "This Girl Got in Trouble at School for Not Wearing a Bra." *Teen Vogue*. Condé Nast, 7 June 2016. Web. 17 Aug. 2017.

3. Li Zhou. "The Sexism of School Dress Codes." *The Atlantic*. Atlantic Monthly Group, 20 Oct. 2015. Web. 17 Aug. 2017.

4. Kaitlyn Juvik, as told to Sam Levin. "Why I Organized a 'No Bra Day' at My High School." *Guardian*. Guardian News and Media Limited, 17 June 2016. Web. 17 Aug. 2017.

5. Cathy Free. "Montana Teen Stages Protest After School Demands She Wear Bra: 'I Was Told a Male Teacher Had Complained He Was Uncomfortable.'" *People*. Time, 8 June 2016. Web. 17 Aug. 2017.

6. Liam Stack. "After Barring Girls for Leggings, United Airlines Defends Decision." *New York Times*. New York Times Company, 26 Mar. 2017. Web. 17 Aug. 2017.

7. Ibid.

8. Kaitlyn Juvik, as told to Sam Levin. "Why I Organized a 'No Bra Day' at My High School." *Guardian*. Guardian News and Media Limited, 17 June 2016. Web. 17 Aug. 2017.

9. Sam Escobar. "This High School's Ban on Natural Hairstyles Is Sparking Outrage." *Good Housekeeping*. Hearst Communications, 2 Aug. 2016. Web. 17 Aug. 2017.

CHAPTER 2. WHAT IS "GIRL STUFF"?

1. Anna Bessendorf. "From Cradle to Cane: The Cost of Being a Female Consumer." *NYC*. City of New York, Dec. 2015. Web. 17 Aug. 2017.

2. Maria Guido. "Target to Stop Separating 'Girl' and 'Boy' Toys, Some People Are Pissed." *Scary Mommy*. Scary Mommy, n.d. Web. 17 Aug. 2017.

3. Samantha Grossman. "2015 Will Be the Year of the Gender-Neutral Baby Name." *Time*. Time, 23 June 2015. Web. 17 Aug. 2017.

4. "Girls Feel They Must 'Play Dumb' to Please Boys." *Warwick*. University of Warwick, 5 Aug. 2014. Web. 17 Aug. 2017.

5. Tara Culp-Ressler. "Forcing Kids to Stick to Gender Roles Can Actually Be Harmful to Their Health." *ThinkProgress*. ThinkProgress, 7 Aug. 2014. Web. 17 Aug. 2017.

CHAPTER 3. SELF-ESTEEM & BODY IMAGE

1. "Body Image & Nutrition." *Teen Health and the Media*. University of Washington, n.d. Web. 17 Aug. 2017.

2. Stacy L. Smith, Marc Choueiti, Ashley Prescott, and Katherine Pieper. "Gender Roles & Occupations: A Look at Character Attributes and Job-Related Aspirations in Film and Television." *Geena Davis Institute on Gender in Media*. Geena Davis Institute on Gender in Media, n.d. Web. 17 Aug. 2017.

3. "Eating Disorders." *PBS*. KCTS Television, n.d. Web. 17 Aug. 2017.

4. "Daily Media Use among Children and Teens Up Dramatically from Five Years Ago." *KFF*. Kaiser Family Foundation, 20 Jan. 2010. Web. 17 Aug. 2017.

5. Scott A. Baldwin and John P. Hoffmann. "The Dynamics of Self-Esteem: A Growth-Curve Analysis." *Journal of Youth and Adolescence* 31.2 (2002). Print.

6. Linda C. Andrist. "Media Images, Body Dissatisfaction, and Disordered Eating in Adolescent Women." *American Journal of Maternal Child Nursing* 28.2 (2003). Print.

7. Dianne Neumark-Sztainer, et al. "Obesity, Disordered Eating, and Eating Disorders in a Longitudinal Study of Adolescents: How Do Dieters Fare 5 Years Later?" *Journal of the American Dietetic Association* 106.4 (2006): 559–568. Print.

8. Jenna Sauers. "World's Top Fashion Weeks Nearly 90% White." *Jezebel*. Gizmodo Media Group, 12 Mar. 2013. Web. 17 Aug. 2017.

9. "Study: Young Women with Sexy Social Media Photos Seen as Less Competent." *Oregon State University*. Oregon State University, 14 July 2014. Web. 17 Aug. 2017.

10. Ibid.

11. Ibid.

CHAPTER 4. GENDER-BASED VIOLENCE

1. "The 2015 National School Climate Survey." *GLSEN*. GLSEN, n.d. Web. 17 Aug. 2017.

2. Gabe Murchison. "New CDC Data: LGB Teens Face Startling Rates of Violence, Bullying and Suicidality." *Human Rights Campaign*. Human Rights Campaign, 11 Aug. 2016. Web. 17 Aug. 2017.

3. Ann P. Haas, Phillip L. Rodgers, and Jody L. Herman. "Suicide Attempts among Transgender and Gender Non-Conforming Adults." *The Williams Institute*. The Williams Institute, Jan. 2014. Web. 17 Aug. 2017.

4. "Hollaback! Releases US Data on Street Harassment!" *Hollaback!* Hollaback!, 17 Apr. 2015. Web. 17 Aug. 2017.

5. "Street Harassment Statistics." *Cornell University*. Cornell University, 17 Apr. 2015. Web. 17 Aug. 2017.

6. "Raising Awareness about Sexual Abuse Facts and Statistics." *National Sex Offender Public Registry*. US Department of Justice, n.d. Web. 17 Aug. 2017.

7. David Finkelhor, et al. "Children's Exposure to Violence: A Comprehensive National Survey." *National Criminal Justice Reference Service*. US Department of Justice, Oct. 2009. Web. 17 Aug. 2017.

8. Laura Kann, et al. "Youth Risk Surveillance—United States, 2015." *Centers for Disease Control and Prevention*. US Department of Health & Human Services, 10 June 2016. Web. 17 Aug. 2017.

9. Ashley Fantz. "Outrage over 6-Month Sentence for Brock Turner in Stanford Rape Case." *CNN*. Cable News Network, 7 June 2016. Web. 17 Aug. 2017.

10. Howard N. Snyder. "Sexual Assault of Young Children as Reported to Law Enforcement: Victim, Incident, and Offender Characteristics." *Bureau of Justice Statistics*. US Department of Justice, July 2000. Web. 17 Aug. 2017.

11. "Teen Dating Violence as a Public Health Issue." *Children's Safety Network*. Education Development Center, Feb. 2012. Web. 17 Aug. 2017.

SOURCE NOTES
CONTINUED

12. "Teen Violence." *Safe Space.* Safe Space, n.d. Web. 17 Aug. 2017.

13. Ashley Fantz. "Outrage over 6-Month Sentence for Brock Turner in Stanford Rape Case." *CNN.* Cable News Network, 7 June 2016. Web. 17 Aug. 2017.

CHAPTER 5. FRIENDS OR FRENEMIES?

1. Melissa Dahl. "A New Study Explains Why You and Your 7th-Grade Best Friend Drifted Apart." *Science of Us.* New York Media, 30 July 2015. Web. 17 Aug. 2017.

2. Rachel Simmons. "From BFF to 'Friend Divorce:' The 5 Truths We Should Teach Our Girls about Friendship." *Time.* Time, 18 Dec. 2014. Web. 17 Aug. 2017.

3. Ibid.

4. Ibid.

5. Amanda Lenhart. "Teens, Technology and Friendships." *Pew Research Center.* Pew Research Center, 6 Aug. 2015. Web. 17 Aug. 2017.

6. "73% of Teens Have Access to a Smartphone; 15% Have Only a Basic Phone." *Pew Research Center.* Pew Research Center, 8 Apr. 2015. Web. 17 Aug. 2017.

7. Caitlin Gibson. "The Disconnected: Low-Income Teen-Agers Miss Out on Social Opportunities because They Lack Technology." *Hutchinson News.* GateHouse Media, 6 Sept. 2016. Web. 17 Aug. 2017.

8. Amanda Lenhart. "Teens, Technology and Friendships." *Pew Research Center.* Pew Research Center, 6 Aug. 2015. Web. 17 Aug. 2017.

9. Ibid.

10. Ibid.

11. "Cyberbullying Triples According to New McAfee '2014 Teens and the Screen Study.'" *McAfee.* McAfee, 3 June 2014. Web. 17 Aug. 2017.

12. "HS Graduates Remember Classmate Who Was Still Bullied after Suicide." *ABC.* ABC, 30 May 2017. Web. 17 Aug. 2017.

13. Ibid.

CHAPTER 6. NOT ALL GIRLS ARE PRO-GIRL

1. Naomi Wolf, et al. "Sexism and Misogyny: What's the Difference?" *Guardian.* Guardian News and Media, 17 Oct. 2012. Web. 17 Aug. 2017.

2. Linton Weeks. "American Women Who Were Anti-Suffragettes." *NPR.* NPR, 22 Oct. 2015. Web. 17 Aug. 2017.

3. Alia E. Dastagir. "You're Sexist. And So Am I." *USA Today.* USA Today, 23 Mar. 2017. Web. 17 Aug. 2017.

4. Talia Baurer. "Do You Fall for the Myth of the 'Different Girl'?" *HelloFlo.* HelloFlo, 17 Feb. 2016. Web. 17 Aug. 2017.

5. Ibid.

6. Stephanie Rosenbloom. "The Taming of the Slur." *New York Times.* New York Times Company, 13 July 2006. Web. 17 Aug. 2017.

7. Ibid.

8. Sheryl Sandberg and Adam Grant. "Sheryl Sandberg on the Myth of the Catty Woman." *New York Times.* New York Times Company, 23 June 2016. Web. 17 Aug. 2017.

9. "Leaning Out." *Harvard Graduate School of Education*. President and Fellows of Harvard College, n.d. Web. 17 Aug. 2017.

10. Sheryl Sandberg and Adam Grant. "Sheryl Sandberg on the Myth of the Catty Woman." *New York Times*. New York Times Company, 23 June 2016. Web. 17 Aug. 2017.

11. Ibid.

CHAPTER 7. YOU'RE PRETTIER WHEN YOU SMILE

1. Kelly Wallace. "How to Teach Girls to Be Confident #LikeAGirl." *CNN*. Cable News Network, 9 July 2015. Web. 17 Aug. 2017.

2. Alina Agha. "Young Girls Deserve to Know They Too Can Succeed." *Daily Texan*. Student Media, 31 Jan. 2017. Web. 17 Aug. 2017.

3. Diane Mapes. "Why Woman Are Terrible at Accepting Compliments." *Today*. NBC Universal, 21 July 2013. Web. 17 Aug. 2017.

4. Ibid.

5. Martha Beck. "Are You Addicted to Praise?" *CNN*. Cable News Network, 29 Jan. 2016. Web. 17 Aug. 2017.

6. Katherine Reynolds Lewis. "How to Stop Being a Praise Junkie." *Fortune*. Time, 10 July 2013. Web. 17 Aug. 2017.

CHAPTER 8. TODAY'S GIRLS, TOMORROW'S WOMEN

1. Kaitlyn Juvik, as told to Sam Levin. "Why I Organized a 'No Bra Day' at My High School." *Guardian*. Guardian News and Media Limited, 17 June 2016. Web. 17 Aug. 2017.

2. Ibid.

3. Mindy Kaling. "Mindy Kaling's Guide to Killer Confidence." *Glamour*. Condé Nast, 4 Aug. 2015. Web. 17 Aug. 2017.

4. "'The OpEd Project' Tells Women to Pen Their Views." *NPR*. NPR, 17 June 2009. Web. 17 Aug. 2017.

5. Lin Bian, Sarah-Jane Leslie, and Andrei Cimpian. "Gender Stereotypes about Intellectual Ability Emerge Early and Influence Children's Interests." *Science*. American Association for the Advancement of Science, 27 Jan. 2017. Web. 17 Aug. 2017.

6. Juliet Perry and Meera Senthilingam. "Girls Feel Less 'Smart' Than Boys by Age 6, Research Says." *CNN*. Cable News Network, 27 Jan. 2017. Web. 17 Aug. 2017.

7. Ibid.

8. "Chapter 1. Elementary and Secondary Mathematics and Science Education." *National Science Board*. National Science Foundation, n.d. Web. 17 Aug. 2017.

INDEX

ABOUT THE AUTHORS

DUCHESS HARRIS, JD, PHD

Professor Harris is the chair of the American Studies Department at Macalester College. The author and coauthor of four books (*Hidden Human Computers: The Black Women of NASA* and *Black Lives Matter* with Sue Bradford Edwards, *Racially Writing the Republic: Racists, Race Rebels, and Transformations of American Identity* with Bruce Baum, and *Black Feminist Politics from Kennedy to Clinton/Obama*), she has been an associate editor for *Litigation News*, the American Bar Association Section's quarterly flagship publication, and was the first editor-in-chief of *Law Raza Journal*, an interactive online race and the law journal for William Mitchell College of Law.

She has earned a PhD in American Studies from the University of Minnesota and a Juris Doctorate from William Mitchell College of Law.

NANCY REDD

New York Times best-selling author and GLAAD Award-nominated talk show host Nancy Redd is an honors graduate of Harvard University with a degree in women's studies. She lives in Los Angeles, California, with her husband and two children, August and Baby Nancy.